WINE
RACKS

GREG CHEETHAM

MINI · WORKBOOK · SERIES

MEREHURST

CONTENTS

Butler's tray (opposite above left), space filler (opposite above right), pigeonhole rack (opposite below)

Storing wine

Storage conditions are important if wine is to be kept for any length of time, as the conditions affect how the wine ages. Put your wine rack in the best possible place in your home, and you'll know you are doing all you can for your wine.

WHERE TO PUT YOUR WINE RACK

Most households do not have, or need, a special wine cellar, but it is still worth paying attention to how your wine is stored and where you place your wine rack. If you always drink the wine within a few weeks of purchasing it, a small rack can be placed anywhere that isn't too hot or in bright light. If you tend to keep even some of your bottles longer it is worth trying to achieve the best storage conditions you can.

Most homes have a few areas that will provide reasonable wine storage conditions. Possible spots include the area under the stairs, a hall cupboard, an unused fireplace or a basement. Rooms with fluctuating temperature, such as kitchens, are not suitable.

Table wines and ports should be stored lying down so that the cork remains moist. Only wines with metal caps are stored upright.

HOW WINE AGES

Each wine is meant to be drunk at a certain age, when its flavour will be fullest. Wine that hasn't reached this stage or is past its best will inevitably be a disappointment.

The conditions in which wine is stored affect how quickly it will age. Ageing should progress at a certain rate. If the storage conditions are not right the wine will age too quickly, but premature ageing doesn't mean the wine is ready to drink sooner – it ruins it – and keeping a wine chilled below the optimum temperature just prevents it ageing properly and reaching its full potential.

TEMPERATURE

Temperature is the most important factor when storing wine. A cool, stable temperature of 10–12 degrees Centigrade is best, although most wines can be stored between 5 and 18 degrees without adverse effect. It is most damaging if the temperature fluctuates rapidly, as this causes the wine to expand and contract, eventually damaging the cork.

Even wines meant to be drunk chilled should not be kept in the refrigerator for more than a few days.

LIGHT

Light can increase the ageing process in wine, and so wine should be kept in a dark place. Certainly avoid bright light, and don't store wine

As well as storing your wine safely and neatly, an attractive wine rack can enhance the appearance of your home.

close to a window. Wine in light-coloured bottles is most affected, and sparkling wines are more susceptible than others.

HUMIDITY

Moderate humidity is best for storing wine, for although the humidity will not affect the wine itself, too little (below about 50 per cent) will dry out the cork. High humidity is less damaging to the wine, but it can cause labels to rot and make it impossible to identify your wines.

VIBRATION

Some wine authorities believe wines are affected by vibration and so should be stored where they will not be disturbed or subjected to vibrations, such as those caused by passing road traffic, low-flying planes or even very loud noises.

ODOURS

Wine can absorb odours through the cork, so don't store it in a place where there are strong odours or food that may ferment.

This bottle rack fits neatly against a wall or in a corner. Made from myrtle and finished with clear acrylic lacquer, it provides an interesting storage option for a modern setting.

Wine pillar

This pillar holds 16 bottles, but it could be made taller to hold more. The stiles are joined to the rails with wedged mortise-and-tenon joints and are screwed to a flat base.

PREPARING THE STILES

1 Check the timber carefully for visual defects and straightness. Select a best face and mark it. Use the combination square to square a line across the face of the 125 x 25 mm timber close to one end and then all round. Measure and mark off the two stiles, leaving 5 mm between each piece for saw cuts. Measure and mark off the two rails. Square the lines all around the timber and trace over the lines with a utility knife and combination square.

MATERIALS*			
PART	MATERIAL	LENGTH	NO.
Stile	125 x 25 mm solid timber PAR	980 mm	2
Rail	125 x 25 mm solid timber PAR	140 mm	2
Base	150 x 25 mm solid timber PAR	500 mm	1

OTHER: Abrasive paper: one sheet each of 120 grit, 180 grit and 240 grit; six 50 mm x no. 8 countersunk screws; PVA woodworking adhesive; wood filler; finish of choice

* Finished size: 500 x 138 mm (base) and 1000 mm high. Timber sizes given are nominal. For timber types and sizes see page 64.

TOOLS

- Combination square
- Tape measure and pencil
- Utility knife or marking knife
- Tenon saw
- Panel saw
- Coping saw or electric jigsaw
- Electric drill
- Drill bits: 3 mm, 5 mm, countersink, 16 mm spade, 32 mm spade
- Drill press (optional)
- Smoothing plane
- Marking gauge
- Chisel: 18 mm
- G-cramps
- Electric sander or sanding cork block
- Electric router with 6 mm round-over bit (optional)
- Screwdriver
- Hammer

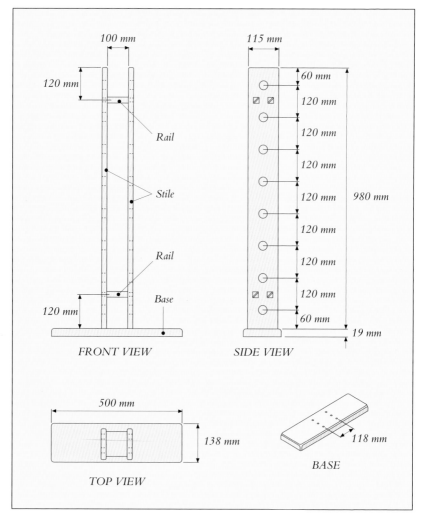

100 mm

120 mm

Rail

Stile

Rail

Base

120 mm

FRONT VIEW

115 mm

60 mm

120 mm

120 mm

120 mm

120 mm

120 mm

120 mm

120 mm

60 mm

19 mm

980 mm

SIDE VIEW

500 mm

138 mm

TOP VIEW

118 mm

BASE

2 Using the combination square and pencil, mark a line down the centre of the face on the stiles. Following the diagram above, measure and mark out on this line the positions of the bottle holes so that they are 120 mm apart and 60 mm from the ends of the stiles.

3 Place a scrap piece of material under the stile so that you achieve a neat finish on both sides. Then, using the 32 mm spade bit, drill the holes at a slight angle downwards (about 10 degrees). Drill one stile as a left-hand piece and one as a right-hand one. Using a drill press with a tilting

base will ensure that the angle of the holes is consistent.

4 With a tenon saw cut all the pieces slightly over-length and plane the end grain back to the knife lines. Plane from both edges towards the centre to avoid chipping out the sides of the timber.

SETTING OUT THE MORTISES

5 On the face side of the stiles measure 110.5 mm up from the bottom and down from the top. and square a line across the face at these points. Use the rails to mark off the thickness of the material, working towards the centre of the stiles. Square the lines across the face, down the edge and over onto the opposite side.

6 On the face side measure out from the centre line 45 mm each way and draw vertical lines between the marks made in step 5. These lines should be 90 mm apart. Measure in from these lines 12.5 mm and set the marking gauge to this mark. Measure in a further 19 mm towards the centre and mark vertical lines to form 19 x 19 mm squares. Repeat on the back of the stiles so you have four squares on each face of each stile.

7 Find the centre of each square by marking the diagonals, and use the 16 mm spade bit to drill holes right through the timber. Use a backing board when drilling.

8 Use the 18 mm chisel to square down the sides of the holes, working to the lines. Chisel down half the depth of the hole, then turn the stile over and chisel out the remaining waste from the reverse side.

MAKING THE TENONS

9 To determine the exact width of the rails, check the distance between the outer faces of the mortises and add 25 mm (it should total 90 mm; see the diagram on page 10). Set the combination square to this width and transfer the width to the rail material. Use the panel saw to bring the material close to width, and smooth the edges back to the lines with the smoothing plane.

10 Hold the rails to the mortises and mark off the size of each tenon on the end of each rail. Number the tenons and corresponding holes, in case the sizes vary. Find the middle across the face of each rail and measure out 50 mm each way from this point. Square lines across the face, edges and reverse side to indicate the depth of the tenons. These lines should be 100 mm apart. Set a marking gauge to the marks on the ends. Next, mark square lines over the ends and across the faces only to these lines. You should now have two tenons marked out on each end of the two rails. Mark the waste to be removed with a cross. Use the combination square and utility knife to trace over the lines where the material will be removed.

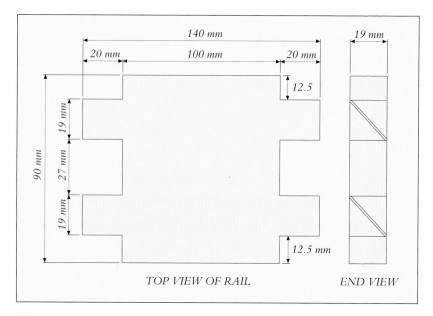

TOP VIEW OF RAIL   *END VIEW*

11 Set a rail end up in a vice or clamp it to a suitable work surface and use the tenon saw to cut down to the 100 mm marks on the waste side of the line. Use the coping saw or jigsaw to remove the bulk of the waste from between the tenons. Clamp the material to a suitable work surface. Use the 18 mm chisel to remove the remaining waste back to the knife lines, chiselling down halfway and then turning the material over and chiselling down from the other side. Cut away the end waste pieces. Check the fit of the tenons and adjust until you achieve a sliding fit.

12 Use the tenon saw to make a diagonal across the end of each tenon, stopping 1–2 mm short of the depth. The tenons should protrude through the stiles by about a millimetre. From scrap material cut eight narrow wedges that can be driven neatly into the end of the tenons. Measure them so they fit the width of the diagonal cuts.

13 Dry-fit the tenons in the mortises without the wedges or adhesive.

ADDING THE BASE
14 Use the tenon saw to cut the base piece to length, and the smoothing plane to smooth the ends square. Measure along the length to find the centre. Measure out 59 mm each way and mark square lines across the face of the base (the lines should be 118 mm apart). Find the centre of each line and measure out from the centre 45 mm each way. These are the centres for the six screws that will

hold the stiles to the base. Use a 5 mm bit to drill clearance holes for the screws at these points. On the underside use a countersink bit to countersink each hole.

15 Dry-assemble the stiles and rails. Stand the assembly bottom up and align the base on the stiles. Use a 3 mm bit to drill pilot holes for the screws. Insert the screws. Remove the screws, pull the assembly apart and sand all the surfaces well with 120 grit abrasive paper.

TO FINISH
16 Round over all exposed corners using a router with a 6 mm round-over bit and ball-bearing guide wheel. Alternatively, you could use a smoothing plane (planing the end grain first and then rounding the edges). Hold the plane diagonally to the end grain with the toe of the plane away from the timber. If preferred, you can leave the corners and edges square.

17 Fill any holes or chips with matching wood filler. Allow to dry, and then sand all the components well with 180 grit abrasive paper.

18 Re-assemble the unit, making sure that the face sides are to the outside and the holes are angled downwards. Use a little PVA adhesive on each tenon. Fix the base into position with 50 mm x no. 8 screws and a little adhesive. Clean off any excess adhesive with a wet rag and chisel.

19 Place a smear of adhesive on each wedge and hammer it into place. Don't hammer the wedges in too hard, as you may split the timber. If the tenons are still loose, use some scrap material to make fine wedges that can be packed around the sides of the tenons to tighten them up. Use a chisel to pare off the excess wedges and a smoothing plane to plane the tenons flush to the stiles.

20 Give the entire unit a final sand using 240 grit abrasive paper and apply your choice of finish.

FINISHING THE WINE RACKS
If burn marks appeared on the timber when you were using a router, clean them off with a cabinet scraper and then sand all surfaces with 120 grit abrasive paper followed by 180 grit. To sand inside curves, wrap the paper around a piece of 25 mm dowel. Make sure you sand in the direction of the grain and always wear a dust mask when sanding. Clean off the dust with a brush.

For the best result apply the finish with a spray gun and compressor, which can be hired. If you don't want to go to this expense, a foam roller will give a good finish. When it is dry, sand again with 240 grit abrasive paper. Clean off the dust with a moist cloth and apply the second coat. For a top-quality finish, apply a third coat.

Made from red-cedar-veneered chipboard and matching timber, this neat unit is designed to hang on the wall, where the bottles will be beyond the reach of young fingers.

Wall rack with drawer

This wine rack holds 28 bottles and has a drawer for corkscrews, coasters and other useful items. The top, bottom and shelves are fixed to the sides with dowels, while the scallops on the rails hold the bottle necks steady.

MATERIALS*					
PART	MATERIAL	LENGTH	WIDTH	NO.	
Side	18 mm veneered chipboard	731 mm	299.5 mm	2	
Top/bottom	18 mm veneered chipboard	700 mm	283 mm	2	
Shelf	18 mm veneered chipboard	700 mm	277 mm	4	
Back	18 mm veneered chipboard	731 mm	723 mm	1	
Front rail	125 x 25 mm solid timber PAR	700 mm		2**	
Front lipping	50 x 25 mm solid timber PAR	774 mm		2	
Side lipping	50 x 25 mm solid timber PAR	319 mm		4	
Drawer front	100 x 25 mm solid timber PAR	698 mm		1	
Drawer side	100 x 16 mm solid timber PAR	275 mm		2	
Drawer back	100 x 16 mm solid timber PAR	683 mm		1	
Drawer bottom	4 mm plywood	686 mm	260 mm	1	

OTHER: 1.5 m of iron-on edge tape to match veneered chipboard; abrasive paper: two sheets each of 120 grit, 180 grit and 240 grit; twenty-four 38 mm long, 8 mm diameter timber dowels; PVA woodworking adhesive; twenty-four 30 mm panel pins; thirty-two 35 mm chipboard screws; wall fastenings

* Finished size: 772 x 319 mm and 732 mm high. Timber sizes given are nominal. For timber types and sizes see page 64. For this project you will need one 2400 x 1200 mm sheet of veneered chipboard.
** Pieces will be cut in half to form four rails.

PREPARING COMPONENTS
1 Use a builders square to set out the parts on the chipboard, leaving a space between each for saw cuts and cleaning up. Read the box on page 33 before you begin cutting. Cut them out using a panel saw or a circular saw and straight-edge. Allow for the 0.5 mm thick edge tape.

2 Plane all the components to the correct size. Use an old iron to apply

TOOLS

- Builders square
- Tape measure and pencil
- Portable circular saw or panel saw
- Tenon saw
- Jigsaw
- Smoothing plane or jack plane
- Old iron
- Smoothing file
- Electric router or rebate plane

- Router bits: 4 mm straight, 18 mm rebating
- Combination square
- Dowelling jig
- Electric drill
- Drill bits: 3 mm, 5 mm, 8 mm, 32 mm spade, countersink
- Marking gauge
- Mitre box or mitre saw

- Two 300 mm G-cramps or quick-release cramps
- Two 900 mm sash cramps
- Utility knife or marking knife
- Chisels: 10 mm, 25 mm
- Hammer
- Screwdriver (cross-head or slotted)
- Spirit level

edge strips to the top and bottom edges of the back panel and to one long edge and both short edges of the sides. Use a file to remove excess edging and smooth the sharp edges with 120 grit abrasive paper.

SIDES AND SHELVES

3 Cut the rebates 18 mm wide and 12 mm deep along the back edge of the side panels, using a router with a rebate bit or a rebate plane. Check that the top and bottom fit flush with the front edge of the sides and the rebate. Adjust by making the rebate wider or planing the top and bottom.

4 On the inner face of the side panels mark out the drilling positions for the dowels (see the diagram on page 16). The first row should be 31.5 mm from the bottom, the next 109 mm up, the others 140 mm. Square the lines across the face. Set the combination square to 50 mm and gauge the distance in from the front edge and the edge of the rebate. You should have 21 dowel positions. Make sure that you have one left-hand and one right-hand side. Mark in the same distance from the front and back edges of the top and bottom panels. Square the marks over the face of the top and bottom panels.

5 On the short edges of the shelves mark in 44 mm from the front for the front dowel positions and 50 mm from the back edge for the back dowels (they should be 183 mm apart). Square the lines onto the face.

6 Using an 8 mm drill bit, drill the dowel holes 12 mm deep in the side panel and 28 mm deep in the shelves. Use masking tape on the drill bit as a depth guide. A dowel-boring bit will give the best result.

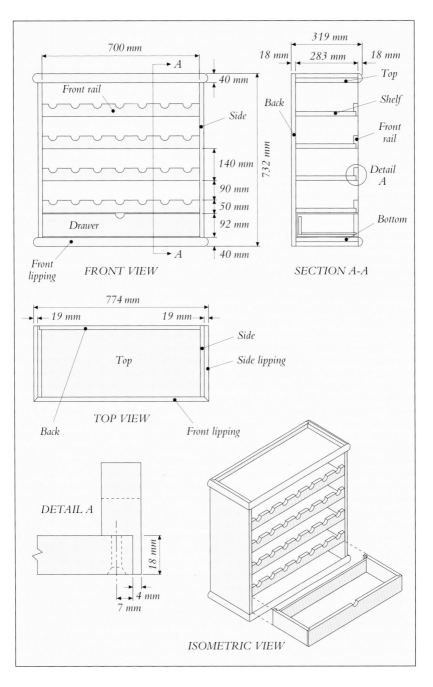

700 mm

A

40 mm

Front rail

Side

140 mm

90 mm

50 mm

92 mm

732 mm

Drawer

A

40 mm

Front lipping

FRONT VIEW

319 mm

18 mm   283 mm   18 mm

Top

Back

Shelf

Front rail

Detail A

Bottom

SECTION A-A

774 mm

19 mm   19 mm

Side

Side lipping

Top

Back

Front lipping

TOP VIEW

DETAIL A

18 mm

4 mm

7 mm

ISOMETRIC VIEW

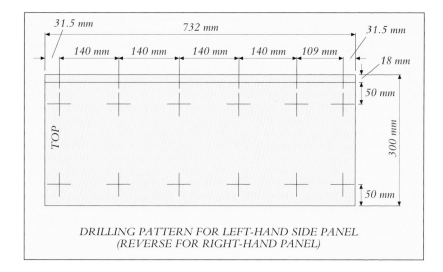

31.5 mm

732 mm

31.5 mm

140 mm   140 mm   140 mm   140 mm   109 mm

18 mm

50 mm

300 mm

TOP

50 mm

DRILLING PATTERN FOR LEFT-HAND SIDE PANEL
(REVERSE FOR RIGHT-HAND PANEL)

7 Dry-assemble the unit to test the fit, and adjust if necessary. The distance from the front of the shelves to the front of the sides should be 6 mm.

THE FRONT RAILS

8 Take the rail material and mark off the two 700 mm lengths, with 5 mm between. On a scrap piece of material, cut a rebate 18 mm wide by 15 mm deep. Check the fit on the front of the shelves to see that the rails will finish flush or just

below the face of the cabinet. When you are satisfied, cut the rebates along both edges of the rail material.

9 Set the marking gauge to half the width of the board and mark a line down the centre of the face. On the centre line mark the centre of each piece. Measure out at 100 mm intervals for the centres of the holes. Place scrap material below the board and use the 32 mm spade bit to drill the holes right through the board.

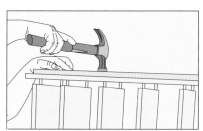

7 Dry-assemble the unit to test the fit. Use a timber offcut to prevent the hammer damaging the surface.

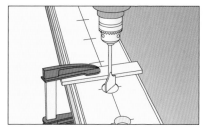

9 Mark the centres for the holes, place scrap material below the board and drill the holes.

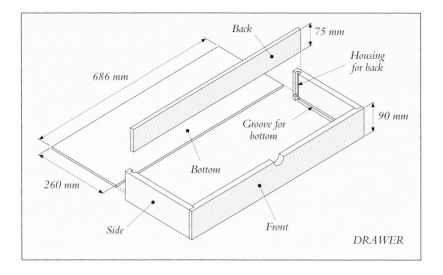

Back

75 mm

686 mm

Housing for back

90 mm

Groove for bottom

260 mm

Bottom

Side

Front

DRAWER

10 Use the mitre box to cut the pieces to length or slightly longer. Plane each back to the marks. Check that the pieces are the same length as the shelves. Use a jigsaw or panel saw to cut down the centre line, creating two rails from each piece. Plane the cut edge to make it smooth. Set the marking gauge to 50 mm and, working from the top edge of the rail, mark a line along the face and the back. Plane the rails back to this marked line.

MAKING THE DRAWER
11 To make the drawer front, cut the ends of the 100 x 25 mm timber square in the mitre box. Plane the top edge to 90 mm and test it for width (it should be 2 mm narrower than the opening). Mark the length of the opening less 2 mm (it should be 698 mm). Trim the drawer front to slightly over-length. Find the centre of the top edge and mark it on the face. Clamp a piece of scrap material to the top edge and use the 32 mm

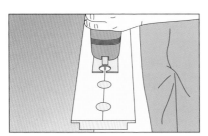

10 Use a jigsaw or panel saw to cut the end pieces down the centre line, creating two rails.

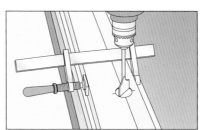

11 Clamp a piece of scrap material to the drawer front and drill a hole at the centre mark for the finger grip.

spade bit to make a hole at the centre mark. You will have a half-circle finger grip in the drawer front.

12 Cut the drawer sides to length. Plane the top edges so that they slide neatly into the opening. Make sure that one end of each is square: these ends will sit in the rebates in the drawer front. Take the front and sides and use a router with 4 mm straight cutter or a plough plane to make grooves 4 mm wide and 6 mm deep, with the top of the grooves 10 mm from the bottom.

13 At each end of the drawer front set out rebates 674 mm apart to match the thickness of the sides. Square the lines across the inner face and 13 mm over the edges. Set up a marking gauge to 6 mm and mark the depth from the front face. Trace over the lines with a utility knife. Use the mitre saw or a bench hook and tenon saw to cut down the rebates to the marked depth. Clamp the drawer front to a workbench and remove the waste with a 25 mm chisel. Check the fit of the sides. (If you use a router for the rebates, be sure to use a backing piece.)

14 Measure in 10 mm from the back end of the sides and then 12 mm (the thickness of the drawer back). Square both marks across the inner face of the sides and over the edges. Use a marking gauge set to 5 mm to mark the depth of the housings from the inside face. Trace the lines with a utility knife. Cut to the depth with the tenon or mitre saw on the waste side of the lines. Remove the waste with a 10 mm chisel.

15 Cut and plane the back of the drawer to 75 mm wide and 683 mm long. Assemble the drawer using PVA adhesive and three 30 mm panel pins in each joint. The drawer should be 1 mm narrower at the back than the front; the back should sit flush with the top edge of the groove. Check the diagonals to make sure that the drawer is square and not twisted. If it is twisted, sit it on a flat surface with a board across the top and stack some weights on it. When it is dry, cut the bottom to the correct size and slide it in the groove. Fasten it with a little adhesive and four panel pins into the drawer back.

16 Punch in the nails at the front and ensure that the ends of the drawer front are flush with the sides. Check the drawer fits in the opening.

COMPLETING THE UNIT
17 Take the unit apart. Use the combination square to mark a line 7 mm in from the front edge of the shelves. Mark screw positions 50 mm in from each end and a third in the centre along the line. Use a 5 mm bit to drill clearance holes and countersink them on the underside of the shelf. Apply adhesive to the rebate on the rail and clamp the first rail to a shelf. Make sure that the ends are flush. Drill 3 mm pilot holes

at the screw positions and fasten the rail with 35 mm chipboard screws. Repeat the process for all the shelves.

18 Use a smoothing plane or round-over bit in the router to round the face edges of the lipping material. Bring it to 40 mm wide. Make sure the timber is straight and parallel.

19 As it will be difficult to reach all surfaces once the unit is assembled, apply the finish of your choice.

20 Re-assemble the cabinet using PVA adhesive. Use two 900 mm sash cramps to pull the joints tight, with padded sticks between the cramps and the unit. Lay the unit face down on a padded surface and check it is square. The back should be fixed on with four screws down each side and across the top and bottom. Then place one in the centre of the second and fourth shelves. Mark the centre line of these shelves on the edges of the side panels. Place the back in position, use 5 mm and countersink bits to drill clearance holes and insert 35 mm chipboard screws.

TO FINISH

21 Mark 45-degree mitres on the side lippings, leaving each 5–10 mm over-length. Cut the mitres. Hold each piece to the side of the unit and mark the exact length, with 0.5 mm overhang at the front. Fasten it from the inside with adhesive and two 35 mm chipboard screws.

22 Lay the unit on its back and measure the width across the face: it should be 774 mm. Take the lipping material and mark off the length, plus 1 mm, along its back edge. With the combination square, mark 45-degree mitres on the ends. Cut the mitres. Apply adhesive to the edge of the top and fix the lipping flush with the inner face using four panel pins. Punch the nail heads below the surface and fill the holes. Apply finish to the filled areas.

23 Try the drawer in the unit. If it is too tight, plane it slightly. If it sticks, rub candle wax or soap on the sides. Fix the unit to the wall with two fastenings through the back at the top and one at the centre bottom.

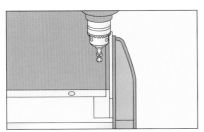

17 Apply adhesive to the rebate on the rail, clamp it on the shelf and drill pilot holes in the screw positions.

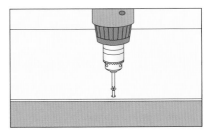

20 Place the back in position, drill clearance holes and insert 35 mm chipboard screws.

Ladder rack

Dowels fitted into frames form the basic structure of this wine rack, which will hold over 90 bottles. Accurate cutting of the many pieces will result in a sturdy, attractive structure.

MATERIALS★

PART	MATERIAL	LENGTH	NO.
Stile	50 x 16 mm solid timber PAR	1441 mm	10
Front/back rail	50 x 25 mm solid timber PAR	856 mm	22
End rail	50 x 25 mm solid timber PAR	208 mm	22
Dowel	10 mm diameter timber dowel	230 mm	176

OTHER: Masking tape; abrasive paper: one sheet each of 120 grit, 180 grit and 240 grit; PVA woodworking adhesive; eighty-eight 40 mm panel pins; twenty 30 mm panel pins; 30 mm chipboard screws

★ Finished size: 880 x 270 mm and 1441 mm high. Timber sizes given are nominal. For timber sizes and conditions see page 64.

TOOLS

- Marking gauge
- Tape measure and pencil
- Combination square
- Circular saw
- Tenon saw
- Mitre saw (optional)
- Smoothing plane
- Utility knife or marking knife
- Bench hook
- Hammer
- Dowelling jig (optional)
- Electric drill
- Drill bits: 3 mm, 10 mm, countersink
- Drill press (optional)
- G-cramps or quick-release cramps
- Screwdriver (cross-head or slotted), battery-operated if possible
- Electric sander or cork sanding block

CUTTING COMPONENTS

1 Take the timber for four stiles, set a marking gauge to 29 mm and mark lines from one end of the timber to the other. Trim the lengths to size, using a tenon saw or a circular saw with a rip guide set to the same width. Use a jack plane to smooth the rough-sawn edges back to the line. The other stiles are 41 mm wide.

This simple rack was made from kauri pine and given a distressed finish, which was then coated with wax and buffed to a soft sheen.

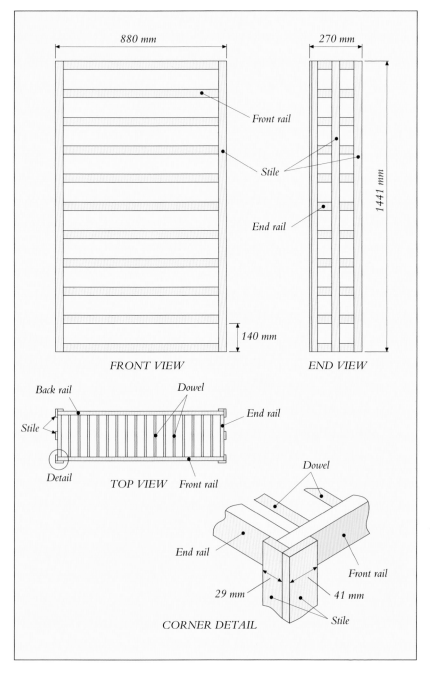

880 mm

270 mm

Front rail

Stile

1441 mm

End rail

140 mm

FRONT VIEW

END VIEW

Back rail

Dowel

End rail

Stile

Detail

TOP VIEW   Front rail

Dowel

End rail

Front rail

29 mm

41 mm

Stile

CORNER DETAIL

2 Cut all the stiles to length with the tenon saw and mitre box or a mitre saw. If you are going to use a tenon saw and bench hook, use the combination square and utility knife to score the lines around the timber faces and edges.

3 Cut the front and back rails to 856 mm in the same way and then cut the end rails.

4 Cut the dowels. You can cut several pieces of dowel at the same time if you bind them together with masking tape.

PREPARING THE RAILS
5 Take four front/back rails and clamp them together edge to edge with the ends flush and square to each other. Measure in 53 mm from one end and then measure off sixteen 50 mm intervals. There should be 53 mm left at the other end. Square the lines across all four rails. Repeat this step until all the rails have been marked out. Set a marking gauge and gauge a line down the middle of the inner face of each rail to mark the

Two stiles form each of the corners into which the shelves are fixed.

dowel positions. Alternatively, you can make a drilling jig from a scrap piece of same-size material that sits over the rails. This means you only have to mark out the positions once accurately. It also helps to put fences and stops of scrap timber or plywood on each end and side of the jig.

6 Use a 10 mm drill bit to make 11 mm deep holes on the inner faces of the rails at the points marked.

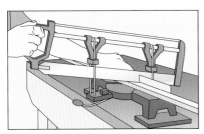

2 Measure and cut all the stiles to length, using a tenon saw and mitre box or a mitre saw as shown here.

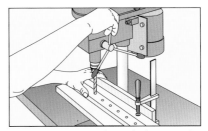

6 Drill 11 mm deep holes on the inner faces of the rails at the points marked for the dowels.

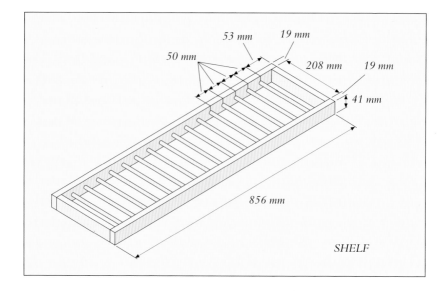

53 mm

19 mm

50 mm

208 mm   19 mm

41 mm

856 mm

SHELF

A piece of masking tape around the bit can act as a depth guide.

7 Sand all the components well with 120 grit abrasive paper and then 180 grit, removing the sharp edges.

PREPARING THE FRAMES AND CORNERS

8 Take one front rail and an end rail. Attach an end rail flush with each end of the front rail. Use a little PVA

adhesive in the joint and two 40 mm panel pins to hold the front rail to the end rails. Apply a little adhesive to each dowel hole and insert the dowels. Also add a little adhesive to the ends of the end rails and the dowel holes in the back rail. Align the dowels and the back rail. If the rails want to stay apart use a 300 mm G-cramp or a quick-release cramp to add some pressure. Repeat for all eleven shelves. Make sure that all the

8 Apply adhesive to the dowels and to the dowel holes in the back rail, and insert the dowels into the back rail.

11 Fix the top and bottom shelves to the rear corners, aligning the top shelves with the ends of the stiles.

shelves are square (measure the diagonals and adjust if necessary).

9 While the shelves are drying, assemble the corners using one 41 mm wide stile and another 29 mm wide stile for each corner (see the diagram on page 22). Apply adhesive and use five 30 mm panel pins to fix each corner. Set them aside to dry.

10 Apply the finish to the shelves and other components. (It is easier to do this before they are assembled.)

FINAL ASSEMBLY

11 Make two 250 x 99 mm spacers. Place a rear corner on a suitable work surface, apply a little adhesive and align the top shelf with the top of the corner. Clamp it in place and use a 3 mm drill bit to make a pilot hole for the 30 mm screw through the frame and into the corner. If you are using a hard timber, drill a clearance hole. Insert the screw into the frame and tighten it until the head is flush with the timber surface. Repeat for the opposite rear corner. Use the spacer to position the next shelf and continue until all the shelves have been fixed into position on the two back corners.

12 Measure along the ends of the top and bottom shelves and mark the centre of each. Align the middle of a centre stile with these marks and clamp it in position. Ensure that the top frame is square in both directions and fix the centre stile to

the top and bottom shelves. Using the spacer, ensure that the next frame is accurately positioned and then fix it in place using 30 mm screws. Repeat the process until all the shelves have been fastened on one side. Then fasten the centre stile to the opposite side of the shelves.

13 Apply a little adhesive to the shelves where the front corners will be attached. Check the shelves for square. Clamp the corners into position, and fasten the top and bottom shelves. Turn the unit face down and fasten all the shelves using the spacer. The screw heads will be less noticeable if you fix the shelves from the underside.

14 Leave the unit to dry overnight, then touch up any areas that may have been damaged during assembly.

USING A MITRE SAW

In this project there are 230 pieces, many of which are the same size. A mitre saw will make the cutting much easier, and you are advised to hire one for a day if you don't already have one.

To improve the quality and accuracy of your cutting you can set up the mitre saw with a piece of scrap material below the timber and a fence behind it to reduce chipping-out. The scrap material can be held in place with masking tape.

This neat rack was made from boxwood-veneered chipboard with matching solid timber for the lippings, and was then given a clear lacquer finish.

Pigeonhole rack

The shelves and divisions of this rack are slotted together with halving joints to form a strong structure. It holds 48 bottles and weighs over 84 kg when fully loaded. Fix it carefully to the wall (it is not recommended for metal-framed walls).

MATERIALS★					
PART	MATERIAL	LENGTH	WIDTH	NO.	
Top/bottom	17 mm veneered chipboard	1020 mm	226 mm	2	
End	17 mm veneered chipboard	806 mm	243 mm	2	
Back	17 mm veneered chipboard	1040 mm	806 mm	1	
Shelf	13 mm veneered chipboard	1019 mm	222 mm	5	
Division	13 mm veneered chipboard	749 mm	222 mm	7	
Vertical lipping	50 x 25 mm timber PAR	807 mm		2	
Horizontal lipping	50 x 25 mm timber PAR	1053 mm		2	
Subframe stile	50 x 25 mm timber PAR	1020 mm		2	
Subframe rail	50 x 25 mm timber PAR	142 mm		5	
Ledger	50 x 25 mm timber PAR	1053 mm		1	

OTHER: 12 m iron-on edge tape to match chipboard; masking tape; twelve 50 mm long, 8 mm diameter dowels; eighteen 40 mm chipboard screws; two 75 mm x no. 10 screws for ledger; thirty 25 mm panel pins; PVA woodworking adhesive; abrasive paper: two sheets each of 120 grit, 180 grit and 240 grit; wall fastenings; finish of choice

★ Finished size: 1054 x 260 mm and 807 mm high. Timber sizes given are nominal (see page 64). The sizes given above are cutting sizes; allowances have been made for edge tape. You will need one 2400 x 1200 mm sheet each of 17 mm and 13 mm veneered chipboard.

PREPARING COMPONENTS

1 Cut and plane the pieces to size (see box on page 33). Apply edging tape with an iron, using clean paper between the iron and veneer to prevent scorching. Also apply tape to both short ends of the end pieces, one long edge of each shelf and each division, and both long edges of the back. File off any excess strip.

TOOLS

- Tape measure and pencil
- Circular saw or panel saw
- Tenon saw
- Smoothing plane or jack plane
- Utility knife or marking knife
- Old iron
- Smoothing file

- Portable electric router
- Straight router bits: 13 mm, 18 mm
- Marking gauge
- Combination square
- Electric drill
- Drill bits: 3 mm, 5 mm, 8 mm, countersink
- Dowelling jig (optional)

- Two 1350 mm sash cramps
- Three 300 mm G-cramps or quick-release cramps
- Screwdriver (cross-head or slotted)
- Mitre box
- Orbital sander or cork sanding block
- Spirit level

2 Mark out and cut the jigs for routing the halving joints in the shelves and divisions (see diagram on page 30). The centre-to-centre measurements are 123 mm (to make 110 mm openings for the bottles). The slots are 118 mm long and 13 mm wide (the thickness of the board). Modify the jig to suit your router. Use a piece of scrap material to test the jigs before routing the divisions and shelves.

3 Use the jigs and router to cut the slots in the shelves, working from the front edge of the shelf. Then cut the slots in the divisions, working from the back edge. Apply a strip of masking tape over each area where the slots will be cut to prevent the edge veneer chipping out. Replace any damaged edge strips.

4 Take the end panels and cut rebates for the back in one long side. The recess should be 10 mm deep and as wide as the back panel is thick. Check the thickness of the board you are using, as it can vary slightly. The back should finish flush

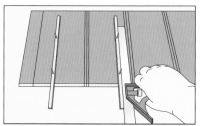

2 Mark out and cut the jigs for routing the halving joints in the shelves and divisions.

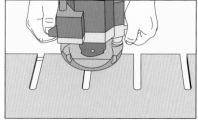

3 Use the jig and router to cut slots in the shelves from the front edge and in the divisions from the back edge.

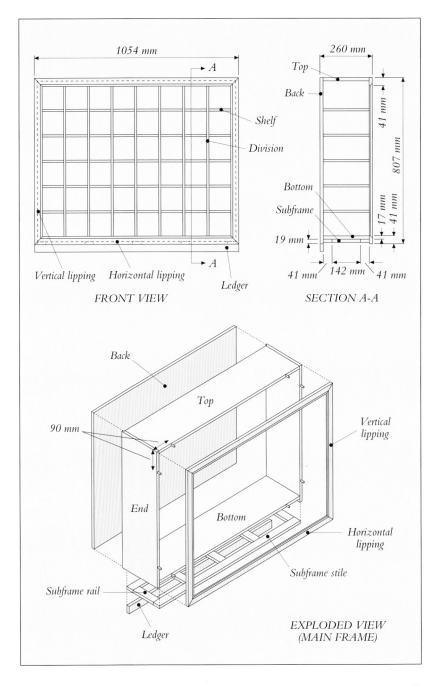

1054 mm

A

Shelf

Division

Vertical lipping   Horizontal lipping

A

Ledger

FRONT VIEW

260 mm

Top

Back

41 mm

807 mm

Bottom

Subframe

17 mm

41 mm

19 mm

41 mm   142 mm   41 mm

SECTION A-A

Back

Top

Vertical
lipping

90 mm

End

Bottom

Horizontal
lipping

Subframe stile

Subframe rail

Ledger

EXPLODED VIEW
(MAIN FRAME)

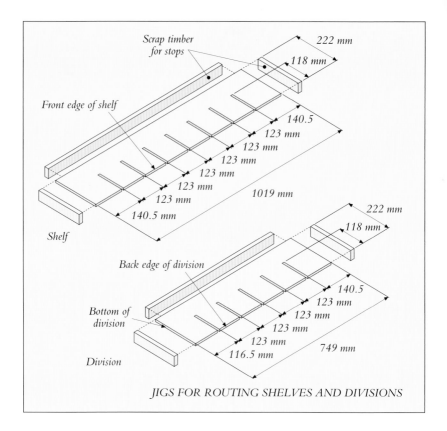

Scrap timber
for stops

222 mm

118 mm

Front edge of shelf

140.5
123 mm
123 mm
123 mm
123 mm
123 mm
140.5 mm

1019 mm

Shelf

Back edge of division

222 mm

118 mm

Bottom of
division

140.5
123 mm
123 mm
123 mm
123 mm
116.5 mm

749 mm

Division

JIGS FOR ROUTING SHELVES AND DIVISIONS

with the edge of the end panels. If you are using a router, test the set-up on scrap first and place masking tape over the edge to prevent chipping.

5 On the end panels use a marking gauge to mark out the positions for the dowels to fix the top and bottom. Position them 8 mm down

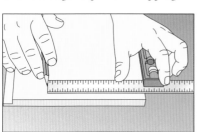

5 Use a combination square to mark the positions for the three dowel holes along the gauged line.

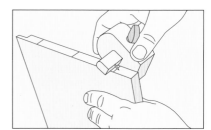

6 Working from the outer face of the top and bottom, square lines across the edge for the dowel positions.

from the top edge and 33 mm up from the bottom edge. Make sure they are set as a pair. Mark the distances from the front edge with a combination square. The first hole should be 30 mm in from the front edge, the second 110 mm and the third 190 mm. Use an 8 mm drill bit with masking tape around it as a depth indicator. Drill the dowel holes 13 mm deep.

6 Establish the front of the top and bottom and mark out corresponding dowel holes on the short edges, continuing the lines over the outer face. Working from the outer face of the top and bottom and using a marking gauge set at 8 mm, square lines across the edge. Set up the dowelling jig and test it on a scrap piece of material before drilling the holes in the top and bottom panels.

7 Dry-fit together all the parts so far. Make sure that the unit is square by measuring the diagonals. Use two sash cramps to hold the unit together while you fit the back to the unit using 40 mm chipboard screws. Drill

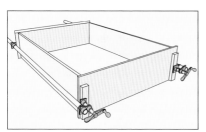

7 Dry-fit together all the parts, using sash cramps to hold the unit together while you fit the back.

5 mm clearance holes and use the 3 mm bit to make pilot holes for the screws. Use four screws evenly spaced down each side and five screws across both top and bottom.

8 Turn the unit upside down on a pair of padded sticks or old piece of carpet to protect the veneer. Cut the subframe stiles to fit between the ends. Glue and nail them in place using adhesive only on the face that comes in contact with the bottom. Cut five rails to fit between the stiles. Glue and nail them in place using 25 mm panel pins. This frame will prevent the bottom shelf bowing when the unit is loaded with wine.

THE LIPPINGS
9 With the cramps still in place, turn the unit face up. Measure in from each corner 90 mm along the front edges. Square a line across the edges and over onto the inside face. Set a marking gauge from the outside faces of the unit to mark a centre line for the dowels for the lippings. On the bottom panel work from the inside face as the lipping is to finish flush with the inside of the frame. Drill the dowel holes 26 mm deep.

10 Mark and cut the side lippings 10 mm over-length. Hold it in place and mark the dowel positions on each. Drill holes 14 mm deep. Check the fit of each piece and adjust.

11 Take one lipping and mark the mitre joints, allowing 0.5 mm more

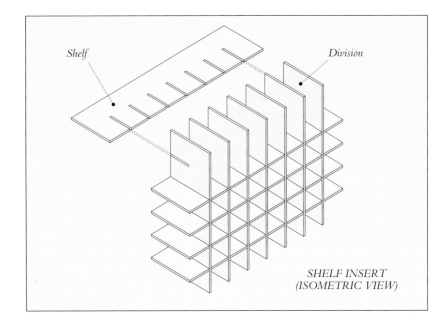

Shelf

Division

SHELF INSERT
(ISOMETRIC VIEW)

at each end. Use a combination square and utility knife to score the lines. Cut them with a saw and mitre box. Glue and clamp the piece to the appropriate edge. Use three 300 mm cramps to get good pressure, and insert scrap material as protection from the cramps. If preferred, use 40 mm nails to fasten the lippings, but punch and fill the holes before sanding and final finishing. If necessary, use a smoothing plane to clean up the faces of the mitre joints.

12 Mark off the mitre lengths on the two adjoining lippings and cut them to length. If the adjoining mitres are slightly open, shave down the dowels with a sharp chisel to get a good fit. When the first lipping is dry, glue and clamp the second in place. Don't

apply adhesive to the ends of the mitres at this stage. For the best results, cut and fit one lipping at a time: mitre joints tend to creep open if you cut and fit them all at once.

13 Determine the fastening points needed to fix the unit to the wall. If it is a framed wall, the position of the fastenings will be determined by the wall studs. Measure out the positions carefully so that they will not be covered by the shelves and divisions. Use at least four screws to hold the unit to the wall, with a minimum of two more fasteners in the ledger. Drill appropriately sized holes through the unit back.

14 Allow the lippings to dry thoroughly before removing the sash

cramps. Take the unit apart. Remove the dowels and sand the lippings flush with the sides (or use a cabinet scraper, which is faster and safer). Use 120 grit and then 180 grit abrasive paper in an orbital sander to sand all the parts. Give a final sand by hand using 240 grit paper in the direction of the grain. Apply finish to all components (see box on page 11).

FINAL ASSEMBLY

15 Lay the end pieces face side down on a clean, dust-free, padded surface. Place a small amount of adhesive in the dowel holes and use a pencil to spread it around. Insert the dowels. Apply adhesive to the dowel holes in the top and bottom, spread a bead of adhesive onto the adjoining edges and assemble the frame. Lay the unit face down (you will need a helper for this) and use the sash

cramps to clamp it together. Check the diagonals for square. Clean off excess adhesive with a damp cloth.

16 Assemble the shelves and divisions (see diagram opposite) and lift them into the frame. Apply adhesive to the rebate and fasten the back in place. Clean away any excess adhesive with a damp cloth. Leave the unit in the cramps overnight.

INSTALLATION

17 Fasten the ledger to the wall so it will sit below the unit, using a spirit level to make sure it is level. For timber-framed walls fix it into the studs with 75 mm x no. 10 screws.

18 Have a helper hold the unit flat against the wall and insert two fasteners through the back near the top of the unit.

USING VENEERED CHIPBOARD

If you haven't previously worked with chipboard, practise on off cuts before beginning the project.

When you cut chipboard across the grain, one side is liable to chip out. Also, if you use a panel saw or table saw without a scribing blade, the under face of the board will chip out. However, using a circular saw will cause the upper surface to chip out. You can reduce chipping by cutting the veneer fibre with a utility knife before you make the cut. Fixing a

length of masking tape across the area to be cut will also help.

Save time and effort by having major parts cut and edged by the supplier (check the telephone directory for one who will do this). Take offcuts away to use later. Buy 1 m of spare edge strip to repair any damage.

Veneered products are prone to becoming scratched easily, so cover the work surface with old sheets or carpet and rest the work on timbers wrapped in fabric.

Butler's tray

This trolley doubles as a storage rack for wine and a serving surface. Ideal for entertaining, it is fitted with casters so it can be moved to the desired location. It holds 24 bottles.

THE RAILS

1 Take the timber for the rails and select and mark the best faces. Cut it into 1050 mm lengths. If necessary, use a jack plane to straighten and square the edges. Clamp the material and cut a rebate 13.5 mm deep and 13 mm wide along both edges.

2 Beginning 2 mm from one end, mark off the rails along each piece, leaving 5 mm between each for the saw cut. Square the lines right around the material and trace over them using the combination square and utility knife.

3 Setting a marking gauge to half the width of the material, gauge a line down the length of all rail pieces on the face side. Use a circular saw with a rip guide or fence to cut along the centre line. Then use the tenon saw, with a bench hook to steady the material, to cut the rails to length. You should have four front rails, four back rails and eight side rails.

4 Set the marking gauge to 50 mm and gauge lines along the length of the rails, making sure that the butt of the gauge is against the rebated side. Use the jack plane to smooth the

---

MATERIALS★				
PART	MATERIAL	LENGTH	WIDTH	NO.
Leg	50 x 50 mm solid timber PAR	750 mm		4
Front/back rail	125 x 25 mm solid timber PAR	768 mm		4★★
Side rail	125 x 25 mm solid timber PAR	268 mm		4★★
Shelf	13 mm veneered chipboard	816 mm	316 mm	4

OTHER: Sixty-four 50 mm long, 8 mm diameter timber dowels; sixteen 30 mm chipboard screws; sixteen 25 mm x no. 6 screws; abrasive paper: one sheet each of 120 grit, 180 grit and 240 grit; PVA woodworking adhesive; four small brass casters

★ Finished size: 850 x 350 mm and 750 mm high without casters. Timber sizes given are nominal. For timber sizes and conditions see page 64. You will need one sheet of 13 mm veneered chipboard for this project.
★★Pieces will be cut in half.

Silky oak was the timber used for this very useful trolley. The rails are' dowelled to the legs, while the shelves are held in triangular mortises.

TOOLS

- Tape measure and pencil
- Circular or panel saw
- Tenon saw
- Smoothing plane
- Jack plane
- Utility knife or marking knife
- Two 900 mm sash cramps

- Three 300 mm G-cramps or quick-release cramps
- Electric router and 13 mm or larger straight bit
- Combination square
- Electric drill
- Drill bits: 30 mm spade, 3 mm, 5 mm, 8 mm, countersink

- Marking gauge
- Dowelling jig
- Bench hook
- Chisel: 12 mm
- Short-handled screwdriver (cross-head or slotted)
- Cork sanding block or portable electric sander
- Hammer

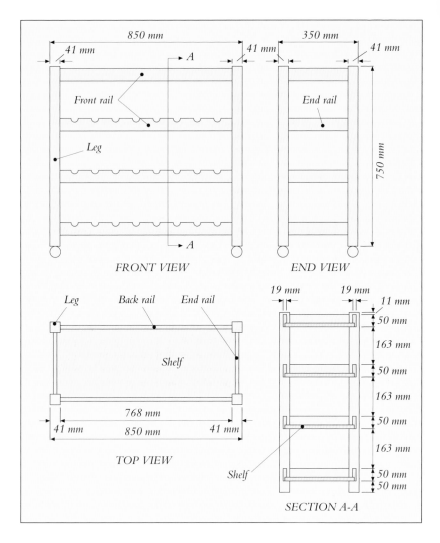

FRONT VIEW

END VIEW

TOP VIEW

SECTION A-A

edges down to the 50 mm marks. Don't plane beyond the gauge lines.

5 Take two front rails and clamp them together face side up and top edges together. On the face side measure and mark 69 mm from one end along the join, then 90 mm seven times, with 69 mm left at the end. Clamp the material down with scrap timber underneath, and use a 30 mm spade bit in the electric drill to bore the eight holes. Take a third front rail and a scrap piece of material the same thickness, and clamp them together. Repeat as for the two rails.

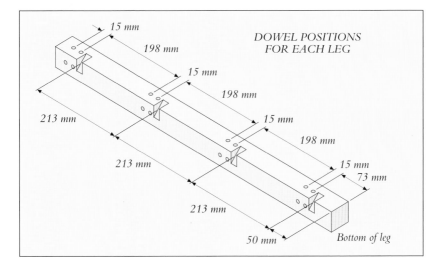

*DOWEL POSITIONS
FOR EACH LEG*

15 mm

198 mm

15 mm

198 mm

213 mm

15 mm

198 mm

213 mm

15 mm

73 mm

213 mm

50 mm

Bottom of leg

THE LEGS

6 Cut the legs to length with a tenon saw and smooth the ends by carefully planing with a smoothing plane.

7 Hold the legs with the top ends up so that only the face sides can be seen. Use a pencil to draw a square on the ends and number each leg. Lay them down with the bottom ends flush and the inside faces exposed. Use a G-cramp to hold the legs together while marking out the dowel holes. Measure 73 mm up from the bottom, then 15 mm, 198 mm, 15 mm, 198 mm, 15 mm until you have the dowel positions for four rails (see the diagram above). You should have 23 mm left over. Square the marks across all four legs. Undo the cramps, turn the legs over so the other inner face is exposed, and square the marks over these faces. Set a marking gauge to 20.5 mm or half the thickness of the legs, and mark the dowel centres.

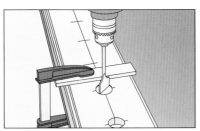

5 Clamp the material and use a 30 mm spade bit to bore the eight holes required for the bottle necks.

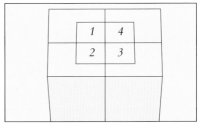

1	4
2	3

7 Hold the legs with the top ends up and use a pencil to draw a square on the ends and number each leg.

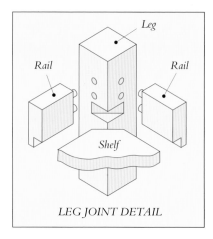

Leg

Rail

Rail

Shelf

LEG JOINT DETAIL

8 Take the four front rails and tape them together with rebates facing the same way and bottom edges aligned. On the ends, measure in from the bottom 23 mm and then 15 mm. Square the lines right across all ends. Repeat for the back and side rails in sets of four. Set the marking gauge to half the thickness of the rails and gauge a line on the end of each rail for the dowel centres.

9 Set the dowelling jig on the end of one rail from the face side to align with the first dowel hole. With an

10 On the inner corner of the legs, mark the shelf mortises in line with the rebates.

8 mm bit drill the holes 30 mm deep in to the end of the rail. Repeat for all rails. Then set the dowelling jig to bore 22 mm deep holes in the legs.

10 Dry-assemble the frame, starting with the two end frames. Set the completed frame bottom up so that access to the rebates is easiest. On the inner corner of the legs, mark the depth and thickness of the shelf mortises in line with the rebates (see the diagram on page 37). Use a square to square the lines across the faces of the material.

11 Take the frame apart. Use a combination square and utility knife to cut across the grain at the marked lines for the mortise. Hold a leg firmly in a bench hook and cut to the depth marked, cutting on the waste side of the lines. Clamp the leg in a vice or to a bench, and remove the waste from the shelf mortise with a 12 mm chisel. Repeat for each leg.

THE SHELVES
12 To cut the shelves, lay the chipboard across a pair of trestles and mark off 316 mm from the edge. Clamp a straight-edge on the sheet and use a circular saw to make a rip cut to this width. Cut a second piece the same width. Check the panels and, if necessary, smooth back to the lines with a jack plane. Lay the two panels on top of each other. Mark off the length of the first shelf from one end and the second shelf from the opposite end. Hold the straight-edge

across the boards with two cramps.
Check that the cramp is square to the
edge of the material and score the
line with a utility knife. Check that
the shelves are all the same size and
are square by measuring the
diagonals. Clean them up to the
correct size with a jack plane.

13 On the underside of the shelves
measure in from each end 200 mm
and 7 mm from each long edge. At
these points drill 5 mm clearance
holes for the screws that will fix the
shelves to the rebates in the rails. Use
a countersink bit to countersink the
holes so the screw heads will sit flush
or just below the surface of the shelf.

14 From each corner measure 25 mm
along each edge, and mark off the
diagonal cut with the combination
square. Trace over the marks with a
utility knife and cut off the corners.

15 Dry-assemble the frame again,
this time inserting the shelves. Make
any adjustments. Take the unit apart
and sand all parts well with 120 grit
and 180 grit abrasive paper.

ASSEMBLY
16 Adjust the two 900 mm sash
cramps to take the end frames,
allowing for the open joints and
scrap material to be placed at each
end. Apply adhesive to the holes in
the legs and spread the adhesive
around the hole. Insert dowels in the
holes and use a hammer to drive
them in carefully. Apply adhesive to

the corresponding holes in the end
rails and assemble the two end
frames. Place them in the cramps
with newspaper under them to catch
any drips of adhesive. Tighten the
cramps until the joints are tight.
Clean off excess adhesive as you
work, using a wet rag and chisel.
Check the diagonal measurements to
make sure that the frames are square.
If they are not, adjust them by
offsetting one or both of the cramps.
Check that the frames are not twisted
horizontally. If so, packing under one
end of the cramps can help alleviate
some of the problem. Leave the
frames to dry overnight.

17 Assemble the rest of the frame in
the same way. Use a cramp to pull
the shelf to each rail. Make pilot
holes with a 3 mm bit and fasten the
shelves to the rails with 25 mm x
no. 6 screws.

18 Fit the casters to the bottom of
the legs and test them. Give the unit
a final sand and clean off all dust.
Apply the finish, not forgetting the
underside of the shelves.

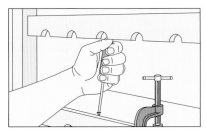

17 Make pilot holes with a 3 mm bit,
and use a short-handled screwdriver
to fasten the shelves to the rails.

This contemporary rack is made from chipboard with sapele mahogany veneer and a clear acrylic finish. The lippings are matching solid timber. Several racks could be placed side by side for large-scale storage.

Shelf rack

Perfect for storing large quantities of wine, this unit is solid and compact. It has 14 shelves, each of which holds up to eight bottles. The shelves are housed into the sides and are finished with solid timber lippings.

PREPARATION

1 Lay one sheet of chipboard across the trestles and, with the tape and square, mark out the pieces. (See the box on page 33 before using veneered boards). If you are going to use a circular saw, fix a long straight-edge to the sheet with G-cramps to help guide the saw. Do a test cut on scrap material and, if necessary, cut the material slightly oversize to compensate for chipping-out. Use an electric plane to bring the panels close to their correct width, then finish with a jack plane. Cut the panels, making the long cuts first.

2 Use an old iron to fix the edge tape to the front edges of the side panels. Then, using a smoothing file remove excess tape, running the file along the edge with a scissor action. Remove any remaining sharp edges with a sanding cork and 120 grit abrasive paper.

3 Cut a rebate 18 mm wide and 12 mm deep along the back edge of

---

MATERIALS★

PART	MATERIAL	LENGTH	WIDTH	No.
Side	18 mm veneered chipboard	1710 mm	280 mm	2
Shelf/top	18 mm veneered chipboard	676 mm	262 mm	15
Back panel	18 mm veneered chipboard	1710 mm	687 mm	1
Lipping	38 x 25 mm solid timber PAR	701 mm		15

OTHER: 3.6 m iron-on edge tape to match veneered chipboard; abrasive paper: two sheets each of 120 grit, 180 grit and 240 grit; matching coloured wax filler; PVA woodworking adhesive; sixty 25 mm panel pins; forty-five 40 mm panel pins; fifteen 35 mm chipboard screws; finish of choice

★ Finished size: 700 x 300 mm and 1710 mm high. Timber sizes given are nominal. For timber sizes and conditions see page 64. Three sheets of 18 mm thick 2400 x 1200 mm veneered chipboard were used, but you could substitute 13 mm or even 6 mm board for the back, although this will require some modification of the rebates.

TOOLS

- Tape measure and pencil
- Combination square
- Two G-cramps or quick-release cramps
- Two 900 mm sash cramps
- Utility knife or marking knife
- Portable circular saw or panel saw
- Tenon saw
- Smoothing plane or jack plane
- Old iron
- Smoothing file
- Cork sanding block
- Electric sander (optional)
- Portable electric router and 18 mm straight bit
- Cabinet scraper
- Hammer
- Fine nail punch or pin punch
- Electric drill
- Drill bits: 3 mm, 5 mm, countersink
- Screw driver (cross-head or slotted)
- Dust mask
- Hearing protection
- Safety goggles

the side panels. If you are using a router, test the cut on a piece of scrap material first. If you only have a small router, make two passes to achieve the correct depth.

THE SHELF HOUSINGS

4 Lay the side panels side by side with the face edges together and the inside faces up, and align the bottom edges carefully. Measure up from the bottom edge 12 mm and 30 mm and mark square lines across both panels. This is the position of the bottom

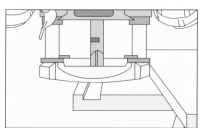

4 Cut the 6 mm deep housing for the bottom shelf using the router with an 18 mm bit and a fence.

shelf. Cut the housing 18 mm wide and 6 mm deep. Set a fence to guide the router when making the cut. Check the settings of the router and the fence to ensure the cut is the correct depth and the fence is set square to the edges. Make the cut from the front edge to the rebate.

5 The gap between each shelf is 102 mm. Measure out the shelf positions accurately and clamp the fence into position for each housing. You can make a jig similar to the one on page 30, which will allow you to repeat the housings exactly but it must be made very accurately. The top will finish 12 mm down from the top of the side panels.

6 Sand all components with 120 grit abrasive paper, being careful not to sand through the veneer. Then sand all the parts with 180 grit paper. Remove the sanding dust and apply

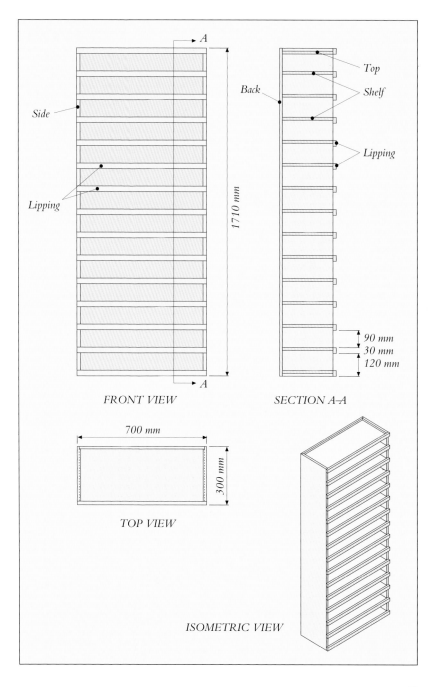

FRONT VIEW

SECTION A-A

TOP VIEW

ISOMETRIC VIEW

HINT

Always use a fence to help guide the circular saw on long cuts, and always check that the fence is set square to the face edge.

---

the finish of your choice to all the components (see the box on page 11). Allow each to dry before turning the piece over and coating the other side.

ASSEMBLY

7 Lay one side panel on a padded surface and apply a little PVA adhesive to the top housing and to the edge of the top panel. Place the top in position, making sure that it is flush both back and front. Working from the upper face, use two 25 mm panel pins to secret-nail the shelf in place. To do this insert the pins at an acute angle. This can be difficult so start the nailing with a hammer and finish it with a fine pin punch. Take care not to put a nail through the side. Repeat for each shelf, working from underneath.

8 Apply adhesive to the housings on the other side panel and a little on the end of each shelf. Put the side panel in position on the shelves and get some help to turn the unit on its back. Take care that the joints don't come apart. Apply sash cramps to the unit, making sure that all the joints are closed up, and use padding to protect the finish. Secret-nail the shelves to the side panel. Remove the cramps. Turn the unit face down on the padding, apply the sash cramps to this side and secret-nail the back of the shelves to the side panels.

9 Check that the unit is square by measuring the diagonals, and adjust if necessary. Mark the centre line of the top and every third shelf on the back edge of the side panels. Set the back panel in place and use a 5 mm bit to drill clearance holes for the screws into the side panels. Use five screws evenly spaced down each side and one screw in the centre of the top and every third shelf. Countersink the holes and use a 3 mm drill bit to make pilot holes for the screws. Insert 35 mm chipboard screws.

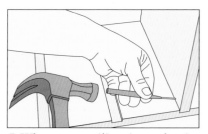

7 When secret-nailing, insert the pins from the underside and at an angle, finishing with a fine pin punch.

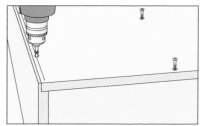

9 Fix the back panel with five screws evenly spaced down each side and one in the centre of every third shelf.

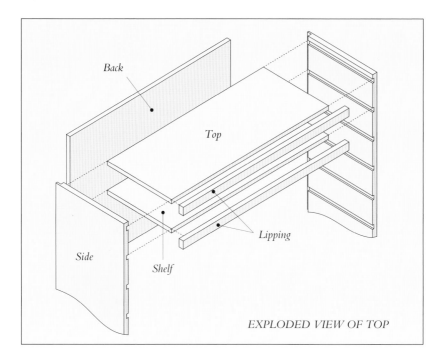

Back

Top

Lipping

Side

Shelf

EXPLODED VIEW OF TOP

THE LIPPINGS

10 Measure the length required for each lipping: it should be 700 mm. On the solid timber mark off the required lengths plus 1 mm. Leave a 5 mm gap between each length for saw cuts. Use a combination square to square the lines all around the timber, and then trace over the lines with a utility knife. Use a bench hook to support the timber while you cut it to length with a tenon saw. Check the fit of the pieces and sand the end grain until it fits the width of the unit.

11 Sand all lippings well with 120 grit and then 180 grit abrasive paper. Apply two coats of finish to the surfaces that will be visible.

12 Apply adhesive to the front of the shelves and use three 40 mm panel pins to secure a lipping flush with the top face of each shelf. You can make a pilot hole in the lippings by cutting the head off a nail and using it in an electric drill.

13 Punch the nail heads below the surface with the pin punch and fill the remaining holes with wax filler.

IRON-ON EDGE TAPE
Iron-on edge tape can sometimes be purchased in 2.4 m strips, but is generally sold in 20 or 50 m rolls. Always buy extra to replace tape damaged in construction.

Wine cupboard

This elaborate unit is a project for the experienced woodworker with a well-equipped workshop. Across the middle is a shelf with let-down door for coasters and corkscrews. The dowel pieces fixed to the front are optional. It holds 80 bottles of wine.

CUTTING THE CHIPBOARD
1 You can either measure out all the components and cut them to size, or have them cut to size and edged by the supplier. If you intend to cut all the parts yourself you will need to have or hire a compound mitre saw able to cut boards up to 300 mm wide. You will also need to use a jointer and thicknesser or planer to machine-dress the components. Use the router to cut out a moulded profile on the skirting material.

2 Apply edge tape to the veneered chipboard. You will need to edge one long side of each of the top, bottom, centre shelves, shelves and divisions. Use a hot iron and a sheet of paper between the iron and the edge to avoid scorching the veneer. Trim the excess edge tape with a smoothing file, using a scissor action, or a cabinet scraper in the same fashion. Use a piece of 120 grit abrasive paper and cork block to remove the sharp edges.

TOOLS

- Tape measure and pencil
- Combination square
- Utility knife or marking knife
- Compound mitre saw (able to cut 300 mm wide boards)
- Circular or panel saw
- Tenon saw
- Jigsaw
- Jointer and thicknesser or planer
- Old iron
- Smoothing file

- Cork sanding block
- Electric sander
- Portable electric router
- Router bits: 6 mm, 13 mm, 18 mm straight bits, bit with a ball-bearing guide wheel
- Hammer and nail punch
- Smoothing plane or jack plane
- Three 300 mm G-cramps or quick-release cramps
- 104 mm hole saw

- Marking gauge
- Compass
- Electric drill
- Drill bits: 3 mm, 5 mm, 8 mm, 32 mm Forstner, countersink
- Sliding bevel
- 60/30 set square
- Mitre box or saw
- Screwdriver (cross-head or slotted)
- Cabinet scraper
- Banister brush
- Hot-melt glue gun

This fine wine rack was made from chipboard veneered with American rock maple and matching solid timber. It was given two coats of white woodstain and then a slow-drying acrylic lacquer with a clear satin finish.

MATERIALS★

Part	Material	Length	Width	No.
Side	18 mm veneered chipboard	1823 mm	281 mm	2
Top	18 mm veneered chipboard	1041 mm	285.5 mm	1
Bottom	18 mm veneered chipboard	1029 mm	285.5 mm	1
Centre shelf	13 mm veneered chipboard	1029 mm	265.5 mm	2
Shelf	13 mm veneered chipboard	1015 mm	262 mm	8
Division	13 mm veneered chipboard	800 mm	246.5 mm	14
Back panel	6 mm veneered plywood	1751 mm	1041 mm	1
False drawer	150 x 25 mm solid timber PAR		969 mm	1
Front skirt	100 x 25 mm solid timber PAR★★		1091 mm	1
Side skirt	100 x 25 mm solid timber PAR★★		319 mm	2
Scalloped rail	200 x 25 mm solid timber PAR		1015 mm	5☆
Front capping	150 x 16 mm solid timber PAR		1140 mm	1
Side capping	150 x 16 mm solid timber PAR		350 mm	2
Side lipping	50 x 25 mm solid timber PAR		1823 mm	2
Support rail	50 x 25 mm solid timber PAR		1015 mm	1
Cleat	25 x 25 mm solid timber PAR		1000 mm	1

OTHER: 12 m iron-on edge tape to match veneered chipboard; abrasive paper: four sheets each of 120 grit, 180 grit and 240 grit; twelve 40 mm panel pins; fifty-seven 30 mm panel pins; sixteen 40 mm chipboard screws; twenty 30 mm chipboard screws; four 13 mm x no. 10 round-head screws; eighteen 25 mm x no. 6 countersunk screws; sixteen 25 mm flat-head nails; wood filler; four handles; two 110-degree concealed cabinet hinges, full overlay type; PVA woodworking adhesive; four 2400 mm lengths of 9.5 mm diameter dowels (ramin timber); four sticks hot-melt adhesive

★ Finished size: 1140 x 350 mm and 1895 mm high. Timber sizes given are nominal. For timber sizes and conditions see page 64. For this project you will need three 2400 x 1200 mm sheets of 13 mm thick veneered chipboard, one 2400 x 1200 mm sheet of 18 mm veneered chipboard and one 1800 x 1200 mm sheet of 6 mm matching veneered plywood. The sizes of the edged components have been reduced by 0.5 mm to allow for the tape.
★★ Moulded timber can be used for decorative effect.
☆ These will be cut in half to make ten rails.

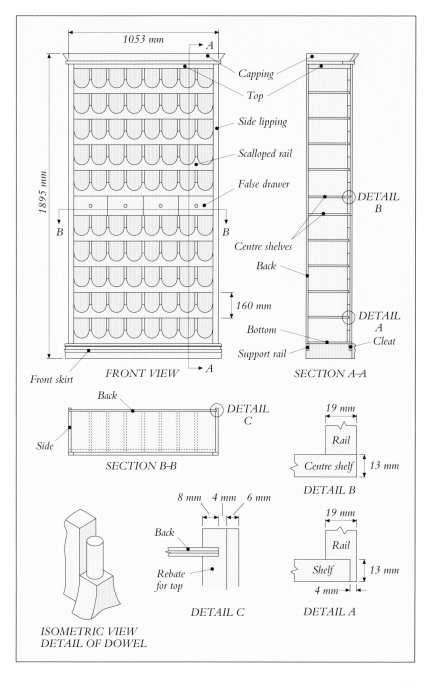

1053 mm

A

Capping

Top

Side lipping

Scalloped rail

False drawer

1895 mm

B   B

Centre shelves

Back

DETAIL B

160 mm

DETAIL A

Bottom

Cleat

Support rail

Front skirt

FRONT VIEW

A

SECTION A–A

Back

DETAIL C

Side

SECTION B–B

19 mm

Rail

Centre shelf

13 mm

DETAIL B

8 mm   4 mm   6 mm

Back

Rebate for top

DETAIL C

19 mm

Rail

Shelf

13 mm

4 mm

DETAIL A

ISOMETRIC VIEW
DETAIL OF DOWEL

THE SIDE PANELS

3 Lay the side panels face down on a suitable work surface, and mark the bottom and the top with a pencil. Measure up from the bottom 72 mm and 90 mm and square a line across both panels. This is the position of the bottom panel. Measure down from the top 18 mm and square a line across both panels for the position of the top rebate. Measure from the bottom 890 mm, 903 mm, 992 mm and 1005 mm. Square the lines across both panels. These are the positions for two shelves. Check that there is 800 mm between the top of the bottom shelf and the bottom of the lower shelf, and also 800 mm between the top shelf and the top panel.

4 Align the two side panels top and bottom. Set the router with the 18 mm cutter in it to a depth of 12 mm. Test the cut on a piece of scrap material. Set the guide fence on the router or clamp straight-edges to the panels to run the 18 x 12 mm rebates across the top of the two ends at the same time. Re-set the guide fences to run the 6 mm housings for the bottom shelf. Change to the 13 mm cutter and move the fences to run the 6 mm deep housings for the shelves. Always test the operation of the router before you make cuts in the veneered board.

5 Set the router up with the 6 mm bit to run a groove down the back edge of the two side panels 13 mm deep and 15 mm in from the back. Use the guide fence supplied with most routers for the task.

6 Take the timber for the side lippings and square one end. Mark off two pieces at 1823 mm, leaving a space between for the saw cut, and cut them to length. Apply a bead of adhesive to the front edge of the side panel, spreading it evenly with your finger. Use six 40 mm panel pins to nail on the lippings so they are flush with the outer face of the panel. Then use a nail punch to drive the nails below the surface of the timber. Set the side panels aside to dry.

THE SCALLOPED RAILS

7 Square the ends of the 200 x 25 mm timber. It should be no less than 184 mm wide. If it is wider than 184 mm use a combination square to mark a line down it, and use the jack plane to plane it to this width. Mark off and cut five rails to 1015 mm. Use the combination square or marking gauge to mark a centre line along the face of each piece. Mark the centre along the line and mark out from each side 61.5 mm. These are the centres for two holes that will form the scalloped rails. Continue to mark hole centres at 123 mm intervals until you have eight hole centres marked on each piece. Use a compass to draw 105 mm circles around each centre mark.

8 Clamp the material to a work surface with a piece of scrap material

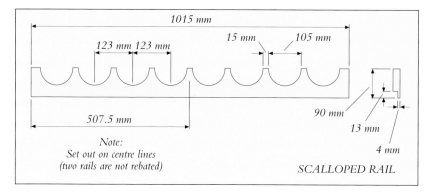

1015 mm

123 mm 123 mm

15 mm   105 mm

507.5 mm

90 mm

13 mm

4 mm

Note:
Set out on centre lines
(two rails are not rebated)

SCALLOPED RAIL

below. Use the 104 mm hole saw to make the holes. Repeat the process until all the holes have been drilled. If you don't have a hole saw this size, most of the waste can be removed using a jigsaw. The remaining waste can be removed with a router template and router bit with a guide wheel or a round sanding attachment for a drill.

9 Choose the best faces of the rail material and mark them. Set up the router with an 18 mm cutter in it and run 13 x 15 mm rebates for the shelves along both edges of four of the five pieces. The rails should be only 4 mm thick at the rebate to cover the front of each shelf. Use a jigsaw, table saw or circular saw to cut each rail along the centre line. Use a marking gauge set to 90 mm and from the rebated edge mark a line across the scallop tops. Use a jack plane to plane all ten pieces to 90 mm wide.

10 Use a combination square to mark the centre of the top of each

scallop down the face of each rail. This will help you line up the nails that hold the rails to the shelf. Apply some adhesive to the rebates in the rails and clamp one in position on the matching (unfixed) shelves. Use a 30 mm panel pin with the head cut off as a bit to make pilot holes. Then nail the rails to the shelves through the bottom of the shelf, in line with the marks made on the face. Put them to one side to dry.

DIVISIONS AND SHELVES

11 The divisions and shelves are joined with cross-halving joints. To make a jig for the divisions, take a scrap piece of material 800 x 250 mm. Check that the edge is straight and the ends are square to the side. Follow the diagram on page 52 to set out the centre lines for the slots. The slots on the divisions are cut from the front edges. At the same time make the jig for the shelves by following the diagram. The slots on the shelves are cut from the back. Test the jigs on scrap board before cutting the divisions and shelves.

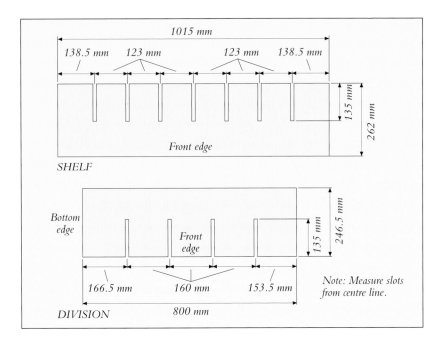

1015 mm

138.5 mm   123 mm   123 mm   138.5 mm

13.5 mm

262 mm

Front edge

SHELF

Bottom
edge

*Front
edge*

135 mm

246.5 mm

166.5 mm   160 mm   153.5 mm

*Note: Measure slots
from centre line.*

DIVISION   **800 mm**

12 Lay a division on a suitable work surface with a piece of scrap material below it. Put the jig into position so you are working from the front edge, and machine the first slots. There may be some breaking out of the veneered edge, but this will only be a problem if the break-out cannot be hidden by the scalloped rail. Replace

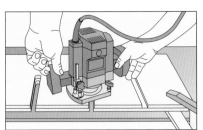

12 Put the jig into position on a division so you are working from the front edge, and rout the slots.

the edge tape if necessary. Repeat the machining for all the divisions. Machine the slots in the shelves from the back edge. Assemble the shelves and divisions and check the spacings.

FITTING BOTTOM AND TOP
13 Lay the side panels out face down on the work surface. Set the bottom panel in the groove hard against the lipping, and on each end mark the cut-out to fit around the lipping (see the diagram on page 54). Use a utility knife to cut across the edge tape to prevent chipping. Return the marks over the face and underside of the panel. Set the marking gauge to the thickness of the lipping, and mark between the existing marks. Set the bottom in a vice or clamp it to a

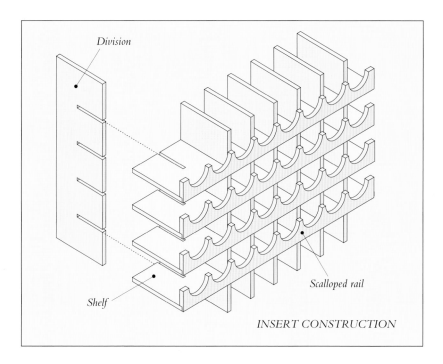

Division

Scalloped rail

Shelf

INSERT CONSTRUCTION

work surface, and use the tenon saw or jigsaw to remove the waste. Test the fit and make adjustments so that the shelf is flush at the front. Fit the top to the sides in the same way.

14 Take one of the two un-rebated scalloped rails, and glue and clamp it to the bottom panel so that it is flush with the cut-outs and allowance has been made for the housing joints. Use five 30 mm panel pins to secure the rail to the bottom panel.

15 Glue and clamp the remaining un-rebated rail to the upper centre shelf. Make sure that the face of the rail is flush with the front edge of the shelf, and allow for the housing.

Secure the rail with five 30 mm panel pins. Punch and fill the holes.

THE FALSE DRAWER

16 Cut and plane the false drawer to the correct size. Divide the face into four equal spaces and square lines across the face. Use a tenon saw to make 6 mm deep cuts at the marks. Turn the panel over, measure in from each end 100 mm, and square a 25 mm line across the inner face.

17 Check the instructions that come with the hinges to locate the drilling positions for the hinge holes. Use the 32 mm Forstner bit to drill the holes for the hinges. Fix the hinges in the holes with the screws provided. On

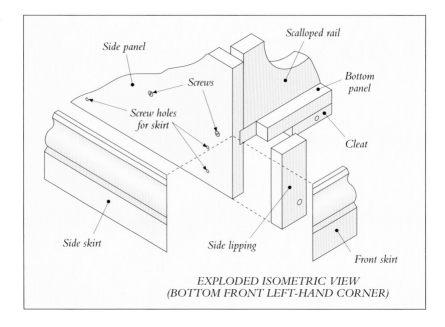

Side panel

Scalloped rail

Screws

Bottom panel

Screw holes for skirt

Cleat

Side skirt

Side lipping

Front skirt

EXPLODED ISOMETRIC VIEW
(BOTTOM FRONT LEFT-HAND CORNER)

the lower centre shelf measure in from each end 130 mm and square lines in about 40 mm. Check that the centres of the hinge arms align with these marks. Fix the mounting plates to the hinge arms and hold the false drawer to the shelf. Use a 3 mm bit to drill pilot holes and fix the mounting plates to the shelf using two 13 mm x no. 10 round–head

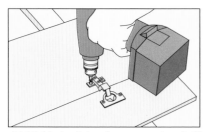

17 Hold the false drawer to the shelf and fix the mounting plates to the shelf, using two screws for each plate.

screws for each plate. Remove all the hardware. On the face find the centre of each section and drill a 5 mm hole through the false drawer at each spot for the handle fixing.

THE CAPPING
18 Take the 150 x 16 mm capping material and gauge a 50 mm line parallel with one edge. Use the circular saw to cut the length into two pieces, one 50 mm wide for the flat capping and one 90 mm wide for the angled capping. Use the jack plane to plane the edges of both pieces straight and square.

19 Set a sliding bevel to 60 degrees using the 60/30 set square. On the end of the 90 mm wide angled capping mark an angle of 60 degrees

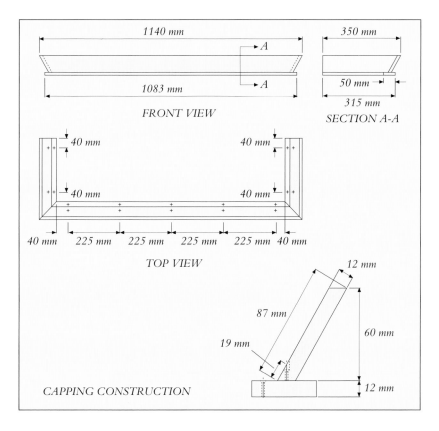

1140 mm

A

1083 mm

A

FRONT VIEW

350 mm

50 mm

315 mm

SECTION A-A

40 mm

40 mm

40 mm

40 mm

40 mm 225 mm 225 mm 225 mm 225 mm 40 mm

TOP VIEW

12 mm

87 mm

60 mm

19 mm

12 mm

CAPPING CONSTRUCTION

from one corner to the face. Set a marking gauge or combination square to the mark and gauge a line along the face. Position the material in a vice and carefully plane the angle down to the line. Set the marking gauge to 80 mm and gauge a line from the sharp top edge parallel with the top edge. Place the material in the vice and plane a parallel 60-degree angle on the opposite edge.

20 Take the flat capping and mark off 315 mm, then 10 mm, 1083 mm, 10 mm and 315 mm. Mark off the mitre joints. With the marking gauge mark a line 15 mm in from the front edge. On the inside face of the angled capping piece mark a line 19 mm up from the bottom. Set the angled piece on the flat piece to align with the 15 mm line; mark the mitre positions on the angled capping. Mark out the drilling positions on the 19 mm line (see diagram above), drill and countersink 5 mm clearance holes. Apply adhesive to the bottom edge of the angled capping and fasten the two pieces together with 25 mm screws. Set aside to dry.

APPLYING THE FINISH

21 The side lippings can be made flush with the side panels using a scraper. This will give you a better finish and remove machine marks and router burn marks faster than using the sander. Also, there is less risk of sanding through the face veneers. Make sure that all exposed nail holes have been filled and are dry. Sand all the parts with 120 grit abrasive paper. Using an electric sander will speed up the process. Take care to sand with the grain and not across it. Sand again with 180 grit abrasive paper. Carefully clean off the dust with a banister brush.

22 Apply the finish of your choice to all the parts (you will get a better result if you do this now than when the unit is assembled).

ASSEMBLING THE FRAME

23 Lay the two sides face up on a well-padded workbench. Set the combination square to 81 mm and gauge a line across the bottom end. Drill three 5 mm holes along the line, one 50 mm in from each long edge and one in the centre. The holes should be in the centre of the housing joint. Countersink the holes.

24 Reset the marking gauge to 7 mm. On the top panel mark a line 7 mm in from each end. Drill three 5 mm holes, spacing them as for the bottom, slightly angled towards the outer edge. This will help prevent the screws splitting the side panel on the inside face. If the angle is too steep the screws may go through the side. Countersink the holes.

25 Turn one side face down and apply adhesive to the housing joint and rebate. Spread the adhesive with your finger to get an even coverage. Apply adhesive to the joining edge of the bottom. Place the front edge of the bottom panel on the work surface and lift the side panel into position. Make sure that the front edges of the bottom and side are flush. Use a 3 mm bit to make pilot holes for the 40 mm chipboard screws, and insert the screws. Insert the top panel in the rebate, drill 3 mm pilot holes and insert the screws.

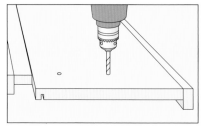

23 Gauge a line 81 mm up from the bottom end of the side panel, and drill three holes along the line.

25 Place the side panel in position, make pilot holes and insert the 40 mm chipboard screws.

26 Turn the assembly onto the side. Apply adhesive to the remaining rebates and housing joints, including the two centre shelves. Insert the two centre shelves, making sure that they are in the correct positions. Lay the remaining side panel on top of the assembly. Align the joints and insert the screws as detailed in step 25. Have someone help you turn the unit carefully onto its face.

27 Make sure that the two centre shelves are firmly in place. If the joints are not coming together tightly you may need to use a 1350 mm sash cramp across the them. This will keep them together while the adhesive sets. Only if absolutely necessary use two 40 mm panel pins to hold the joint together, punching and filling the holes. Alternatively, insert 19 x 19 mm cleats on the underside of the bottom shelf and the top of the top shelf. These will not interfere with the operation of the unit, but they will be visible. Check that the unit is square by measuring the diagonals, adjust it if necessary, and leave to dry.

28 While the unit is face down, cut the 1015 mm long support rail to go under the back of the bottom shelf. Set the combination square or marking gauge to 24 mm. Working from the back edge of the side panels, mark a line 80 mm up from the bottom. With a tape measure, measure up from the bottom 51 mm and 71 mm along the lines. At these points drill a 5 mm hole and

countersink it. Apply a bead of adhesive to the support rail, hold it hard against the bottom shelf and use two 40 mm chipboard screws to fasten it into place.

29 When the main unit has dried, fit the shelves and divisions within it. Slide the back into position and check the unit for square one last time. When you are satisfied, fasten the back to the top and bottom with five 25 mm flat-head nails. Use a straight-edge to mark the centre line of the two central shelves, and use five nails in each shelf. Carefully turn the unit on its side on the padding.

ADDING THE SKIRTINGS

30 Measure the depth of the unit (it should be 300 mm). Take the skirting material and square the two ends with the mitre saw. Mark the width of the unit, plus a half millimetre, on the back side of the skirting from each end. Square the line across the back and use the combination square to mark the mitres across the top and bottom edge of the skirting. Set the mitre

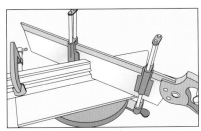

30 Mark the mitres across the top and bottom of the skirting, set the mitre saw to 45 degrees and cut the mitre.

saw to 45 degrees and clamp the skirting in the mitre saw. Cut the first mitre, turn the saw to the opposite mitre, and cut the second. Check the fit. The face length of each piece should be 319 mm.

31 Apply a little adhesive to the back of the skirting and clamp it in place. Make sure that it is flush with the back edge and overhanging the lippings by only a half millimetre. Drill four 5 mm holes through the side panel to fix the skirting, and use four 30 mm chipboard screws to hold each skirting piece in place.

32 Measure and mark off on the back of the material the length of the front skirting, allowing an extra half millimetre overall. Use the mitre saw to cut and fit it as for the side skirtings. Check the fit.

33 Cut the cleat to length. Mark out five equal spacings along two faces so that the screw holes will not clash. Drill at an angle through each. At the same time, drill one hole through the lipping material near the bottom to

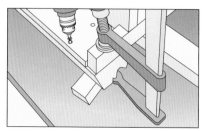

31 Clamp the skirting in place and drill four 5 mm holes through the side panel to fix each skirting.

secure the bottom of the skirting. Apply adhesive and fasten the cleat to the underside of the bottom shelf with five 30 mm chipboard screws. Set the cleat back about half a millimetre from the front edge.

34 Apply adhesive to the mitred ends of the front skirting and clamp it in place. Use a 3 mm bit to make pilot holes through the lipping into the bottom of the skirting at each side for 30 mm screws. If the moulding is thin at the top edge you may need to use a smaller screw. Check before you insert the screws that they will not come through. Stand the unit upright (this may take more than two people, as the unit is very heavy).

ADDING THE CAPPING

35 Stand the unit on the floor. Measure the width and depth: the unit should be 1053 x 300 mm at the top. Add 15 mm to the depth measurement and 30 mm to the width measurement. This gives the lengths of the flat cappings. Measure in along the bottom of the flat capping from each end the length of the side flat capping plus 5 mm. Square the mark to the front edge of the flat capping, and mark out the mitre cut on the bottom.

36 Align the flat capping in the mitre saw so that the mitre mark on the flat capping is lined up with the saw cut in the bottom bed of the mitre saw. Use two G-cramps or

quick-release cramps and scrap blocks to hold the flat capping firmly in the mitre saw, and cut the mitre. Repeat the step for the other mitres. Trim the ends of the side flat cappings to the correct length.

37 On the inside of the flat cappings make slotted holes 40 mm in from each end with a 5 mm drill bit. The front piece can have slotted screw holes put in at the same positions and three plain 5 mm holes equally spaced between. With a smoothing plane make sure the sides are flush with the top panel. Set the combination square or marking gauge to 35 mm and mark a line on the top of the unit in from the front edge and sides. The inside of the flat capping should align with this. Line up one of the side flat cappings, drill the 3 mm pilot holes and fasten the piece into place. Repeat the step for the opposite side.

38 Adjust the fit of the front flat capping to the side flat capping. You may need to loosen the screws and use a little packing to get the fit just right. Remove the pieces, apply a little adhesive to the underside, the flat capping and the mitres, and fix them back into place. Fasten down the screws and insert the remaining screws into the front flat capping.

TO FINISH

39 Measure the length for the 170 dowel pieces (it should be 70 mm). Take time to get the sizes right. Cut

FITTING A MITRE

If you have cut a mitre too long, there is a trick to shortening it. Re-assemble both of the pieces in the mitre saw. Clamp them so that they are held tight together and the blade of the saw is only taking a fine amount off the piece to be cut. The use of a guide or a stop should prevent this problem from occurring.

them and fix them in place using hot-melt adhesive. If some divisions do not line up with the middle of the scallop, cut the head off a 40 mm panel pin and use it as a drill bit to drill down through the top of the scalloped rail at an angle into the front of the division. Use a 25 mm panel pin to hold the division in place; punch the pin head below the surface. The nail hole should be far enough back so the dowel covers it.

40 Put the hinges back on the false drawer front and attach it to the unit. Attach the handles.

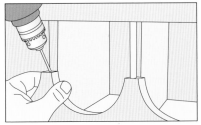

39 Pull the divisions into place by drilling through the rail into the division. Fix with a panel pin.

This easy-to-make unit was constructed of hoop pine and finished with an aerosol spray lacquer, which gets into difficult angles better than a brush.

Space filler

This unit was built to fit into a microwave space, but it could be freestanding. It is easy to make and inexpensive, making it an ideal wine rack for any household. It holds 17 bottles.

PREPARATION

1 Check that the corners of the piece of chipboard or plywood are square. Use the T-square, set square and pencil to set out the dimensions of the space into which the rack will be fitted (600 x 450 mm in this case, but adjust the size to suit). Check that

the shape is square. Use the T-square to find the exact centre.

2 Use the T-square and set square to mark a cross with arms at 45 degrees. On each side of the centre along each arm mark 47.5 mm, then 19 mm, 95 mm and 19 mm until you reach

MATERIALS*

Part	Material	Length	No.
Rail A	25 x 16 mm solid timber PAR	600 mm	8
Rail B	25 x 16 mm solid timber PAR	400 mm	8
Rail C	25 x 16 mm solid timber PAR	200 mm	8

OTHER: 700 x 550 mm chipboard or plywood; 2100 mm of scrap timber (for frame); 1500 mm length of 10 mm diameter timber dowel; PVA woodworking adhesive; forty-eight 20 mm panel pins; twelve 38 mm x no. 6 round-head screws; wood filler; abrasive paper: one sheet each of 180 grit and 240 grit

★ Finished size: 564 x 414 mm and 250 mm deep. Timber sizes given are nominal. For timber sizes and conditions see page 64.

the edge. Use the T-square and set square to fill in the diamond shapes (see diagram on page 62). Cut and nail scrap timber around the edges.

3 Use the set-out to mark off the rail lengths. Use the combination square to make the mitre lines in the right direction and trace over them with a utility knife. Cut the rails.

MAKING THE LATTICE
4 Set two rails accurately in position and pin them to the board in a position that will be hidden by the rails that cross them. Make two

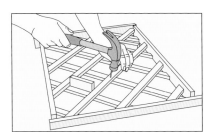

5 Add the pieces for the second layer and fix them with adhesive and a panel pin at each crossing point.

spacer blocks 95 mm wide from scrap material. Measure carefully, as accuracy is important for the final result. Use the spacer blocks to position the next rails. Repeat until the first layer is complete.

5 Set out the two centre rails of the second layer as for the first layer. Use adhesive at each crossing and two

TOOLS
- T-square and 45-degree set square
- Tape measure and pencil
- Mitre box or saw
- Tenon saw
- Combination square
- Utility knife or marking knife
- Hammer and fine nail punch
- Electric drill
- Drill bits: 3 mm, 5 mm, 10 mm
- Screwdriver
- Filler knife
- Cork sanding block

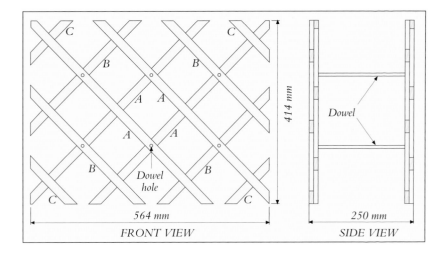

564 mm

414 mm

250 mm

FRONT VIEW

SIDE VIEW

Dowel hole

Dowel

panel pins to hold them in position. Set out and cut the other rails the same way, using spacer blocks to keep the gaps regular. Mark the six dowel positions (see the diagram above). Fix the rails with adhesive and panel pins but don't use pins where the dowels will go.

6 With a 10 mm bit, drill 13 mm deep holes for the dowels. Using a 5 mm bit, drill holes through the centre of the holes.

7 Remove the lattice from the frame and make a second piece the same.

ASSEMBLY
8 Cut six 226 mm lengths of dowel. Position them and fit the rack where it will go. If the rack is tight, mark it and take it apart. Clamp an offcut big enough to cover the part being trimmed to a bench. Push the relevant rails hard against the offcut

and clamp them in place. Trim with a tenon saw. Check the fit.

9 Assemble the rack and use a 3 mm bit to drill pilot holes for the screws. Insert the screws. Take the rack apart.

10 Punch the pins below the surface. Sand the frames and dowels with 180 grit abrasive paper, working in the direction of the grain. Apply the finish of your choice. Re-assemble the rack using PVA adhesive in the dowel holes. Fix with brass screws.

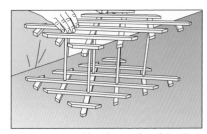

10 Re-assemble the rack, this time using PVA adhesive in the dowel holes, and fix with the brass screws.

Tools for making wine racks

Some of the most useful tools for making wine racks are shown below. Build up your tool kit gradually – most of the tools can be purchased from your local hardware store.

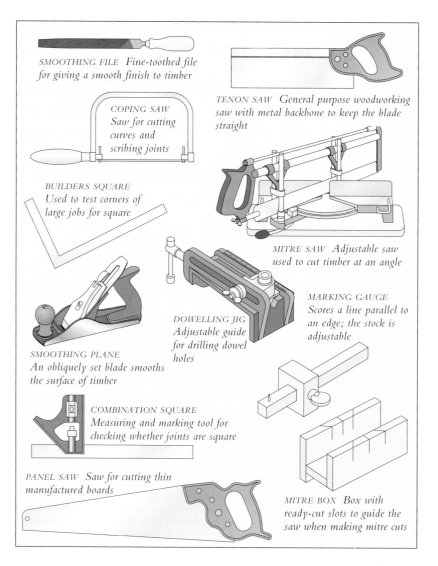

SMOOTHING FILE *Fine-toothed file for giving a smooth finish to timber*

COPING SAW *Saw for cutting curves and scribing joints*

TENON SAW *General purpose woodworking saw with metal backbone to keep the blade straight*

BUILDERS SQUARE *Used to test corners of large jobs for square*

MITRE SAW *Adjustable saw used to cut timber at an angle*

MARKING GAUGE *Scores a line parallel to an edge; the stock is adjustable*

DOWELLING JIG *Adjustable guide for drilling dowel holes*

SMOOTHING PLANE *An obliquely set blade smooths the surface of timber*

COMBINATION SQUARE *Measuring and marking tool for checking whether joints are square*

PANEL SAW *Saw for cutting thin manufactured boards*

MITRE BOX *Box with ready-cut slots to guide the saw when making mitre cuts*

Index

TIMBER CONDITIONS

Timber is sold in three conditions:
- sawn or rough-sawn: sawn to a specific (nominal) size
- planed all round (PAR)
- moulded: dressed to a specific profile for architraves, window sills, skirting boards and so on.

Planed timber is mostly sold using the same nominal dimensions as sawn timber, for example 100 x 50 mm, but the surfaces have all been machined to a flat, even width and thickness so the '100 x 50 mm' timber is actually 91 x 41 mm. The chart shows the actual sizes for seasoned timber; unseasoned timber, such as radiata pine, will vary in size.

Moulded timbers are also ordered by nominal sizes, but check them carefully as there will be variations.

Sawn (nominal) size (mm)	Size after planing (mm)
16	12
19	15
25	19
38	30
75	66
50	41
100	91
125	115
150	138
200	185